GOODSON MUMBA
Educational Psychology
Bridging Theory and Practice

Copyright © 2024 by Goodson Mumba

All rights reserved. No part of this publication may be reproduced, stored or transmitted in any form or by any means, electronic, mechanical, photocopying, recording, scanning, or otherwise without written permission from the publisher. It is illegal to copy this book, post it to a website, or distribute it by any other means without permission.

First edition

ISBN: 9798335683630

This book was professionally typeset on Reedsy. Find out more at reedsy.com

Contents

Preface — iv
Acknowledgement — vi
Dedication — vii
Disclaimer — viii

1. Chapter 1: Introduction to Educational Psychology — 1
2. Chapter 2: Cognitive Development and Learning — 12
3. Chapter 3: Motivation in Education — 24
4. Chapter 4: Classroom Management and Discipline — 34
5. Chapter 5: Diversity and Inclusion in Education — 44
6. Chapter 6: Assessment and Evaluation — 53
7. Chapter 7: Instructional Strategies and Methods — 62
8. Chapter 8: Social and Emotional Learning (SEL) — 71
9. Chapter 9: Special Education and Support Services — 80
10. Chapter 10: Professional Development for Educators — 89

About the Author — 98

Preface

Educational psychology stands at the intersection of how we learn and how we teach, offering invaluable insights that can transform educational practices and outcomes. "Educational Psychology: Bridging Theory and Practice" aims to illuminate this intersection, providing educators, students, and researchers with a comprehensive guide to the foundational theories and practical applications that define this dynamic field.

This book is designed to be both an academic resource and a practical guide. Each chapter delves into key concepts and theories, offering clear explanations and real-world examples that illustrate how these ideas can be applied in diverse educational settings. From cognitive development and learning processes to classroom management and social-emotional learning, the chapters are structured to provide a thorough understanding of the multifaceted nature of educational psychology.

In writing this book, I aimed to create a resource that is accessible and relevant to a wide audience. Whether you are a teacher seeking to enhance your instructional methods, a student studying to become an educator, or a researcher exploring the latest trends in educational psychology, you will find valuable insights and practical tools within these pages.

A special emphasis is placed on contemporary issues and innovations in education. As our understanding of learning evolves, so too must our approaches to teaching. Chapters on technology integration, inclusive education, and professional development reflect the current landscape of education and provide forward-looking perspectives on where the field is headed.

As you read "Educational Psychology: Bridging Theory and Practice," I hope you find inspiration, knowledge, and practical strategies that will enhance your work and contribute to the success of your students. Education is a powerful tool for change, and by bridging the gap between theory and practice, we can create learning environments that empower all students to reach their full potential.

Thank you for embarking on this journey with me.

Goodson Mumba

Acknowledgement

I wish to express my eternal gratitude to the Almighty God for the boundless wisdom emanating from His universal consciousness, which enriches our understanding of the world. I also extend my heartfelt appreciation to all those who have contributed to my life's journey, providing spiritual, moral, emotional, and material support.

Dedication

I extend my sincerest gratitude to my beloved wife, Edith Mumba, and our children, Angelina, Lubuto, Letticia, Lulumbi, and Butusho, for their unwavering support and understanding throughout the conception, writing, and eventual publication of this book, despite the sacrifices and challenges they endured.

Disclaimer

This book is a work of fiction. Names, characters, businesses, places, events, and incidents are either the products of the author's imagination or used in a fictitious manner. Any resemblance to actual persons, living or dead, or actual events is purely coincidental.

1

Chapter 1: Introduction to Educational Psychology

The Catalyst

Evans Roberts had been teaching history at Crestwood High School for over ten years. Known for his passion and engaging storytelling, he had always been a favorite among students. But recently, a sense of disillusionment had started creeping into his once-enthusiastic approach to teaching. The gap between his expectations and reality was widening, and it was taking a toll on his spirit.

The Incident

One crisp autumn afternoon, Evans was midway through his lesson on the Renaissance when he noticed Maria, a bright but frequently disengaged student, staring blankly out the window. This wasn't the first time Maria seemed lost, but today it hit Evans hard.

"Maria, can you tell us why the Renaissance was such a pivotal period in history?" he asked, hoping to pull her back into the discussion.

Maria shrugged without turning her gaze. "I don't know, Mr. Roberts. Does it even matter?"

The question stung more than he wanted to admit. Maria's apathy mirrored the growing detachment he felt from his students. He spent the rest of the class mechanically going through the motions, his mind elsewhere.

A New Opportunity

After class, Evans sat in his empty classroom, contemplating Maria's question. He was interrupted by a soft knock on the door. It was Ms. Lewis, the school counselor, holding a brochure.

"Evans, I thought you might be interested in this," she said, handing it to him. "It's a seminar on educational psychology. I attended one last year, and it was eye-opening. It might give you some new strategies to reach students like Maria."

Evans looked at the brochure skeptically. "Educational psychology?"

Discovering Educational Psychology

Despite his initial doubts, Evans decided to attend the seminar. Held in a nearby conference center, it promised insights into understanding and improving student learning. On the first day, he found himself surrounded by educators from various backgrounds, all eager to learn.

Dr. Linda Chang, a renowned expert in educational psychology, took the stage. Her presence was commanding, and her passion for the subject was evident.

"Welcome, everyone," she began. "Educational psychology is the study of how people learn and the best practices to facilitate that learning. It bridges the gap between theory and practice, helping educators understand the cognitive, emotional, and social processes that underlie learning."

As Dr. Chang spoke, Evans found himself taking notes fervently.

Definition and Scope

What is Educational Psychology?

"Educational psychology," Dr. Chang continued, "is about understanding the learner's mind. It's not just about teaching methods but about comprehending how students absorb, process, and retain knowledge. It's about motivation, classroom dynamics, and the psychological principles that can make or break the learning experience."

Evans was intrigued. He realized that his frustration stemmed from not fully understanding the deeper processes affecting his students' learning.

Historical Development

Dr. Chang delved into the history of educational psychology. "The roots of educational psychology can be traced back to philosophers like Plato and Aristotle, who pondered how people learn. However, it wasn't until the late 19th and early 20th centuries that it emerged as a distinct field, thanks to pioneers like William James, John Dewey, and E.L. Thorndike."

She highlighted how each contributed to the field:

- **William James**: Emphasized the importance of the learner's experience and practical teaching methods.
- **John Dewey**: Advocated for experiential education and the role of social interactions in learning.
- **E.L. Thorndike**: Introduced the idea of measurement and evaluation in education, leading to more scientific approaches to understanding learning.

Key Theories and Theorists

Dr. Chang's lecture continued, now focusing on key theories and theorists who shaped educational psychology.

"We cannot talk about educational psychology without mentioning Jean Piaget, who proposed the theory of cognitive development, explaining how children think and learn differently at various stages of their lives. Then there's Lev Vygotsky, who introduced the concept of the Zone of Proximal Development, emphasizing the role of social interaction in learning."

Evans was particularly fascinated by Vygotsky's ideas. He could see how understanding the social context of learning might help him connect better with students like Maria.

"And let's not forget B.F. Skinner," Dr. Chang added. "His work on behaviorism and operant conditioning has profound implications for classroom management and instructional design."

Epiphany

As the seminar progressed, Evans felt a growing sense of enlightenment. The theories and historical insights provided a new lens through which he could view his teaching practices. He realized that his frustration wasn't just about the students; it was about his methods not evolving with their needs.

Leaving the seminar, Evans felt a renewed sense of purpose. Armed with a deeper understanding of educational psychology, he was eager to return to Crestwood High and start bridging the gap between theory and practice. He was determined to reignite his passion for teaching and make a real difference in his students' lives, starting with Maria.

Importance in Education

Role in Curriculum Development

Returning to Crestwood High after the seminar, Evans Roberts was eager to implement what he had learned. The first area he tackled was curriculum development. He sat in his classroom after school, reviewing his lesson plans with fresh eyes.

Evans decided to meet with his department head, Ms. Johnson, to discuss integrating educational psychology principles into the curriculum.

"Evans, you look different. What's on your mind?" Ms. Johnson asked, noticing his newfound enthusiasm.

"I attended a seminar on educational psychology," Evans began. "It was enlightening. I think we need to rethink how we design our curriculum. For instance, incorporating Piaget's stages of cognitive development can help us create age-appropriate learning activities that align with our students' developmental stages."

Ms. Johnson nodded thoughtfully. "That sounds promising. Let's try incorporating some of these ideas into the next unit plan and see how it goes."

Evans felt a surge of hope. This was the first step towards a more effective and engaging curriculum.

Influence on Teaching Methods

In the following weeks, Evans began to transform his teaching methods. Instead of traditional lectures, he introduced more interactive activities, influenced by Vygotsky's social constructivist theory. He encouraged group projects and peer-to-peer learning, fostering a collaborative classroom environment.

One afternoon, while discussing the Industrial Revolution, Evans grouped his students into small teams to work on a project. Each group had to create a presentation, drawing parallels between historical industrial advancements and modern technological innovations.

To his delight, even Maria seemed engaged, actively participating in her group. She researched the impact of the steam engine on society and compared it to the advent of the internet. Watching her enthusiasm, Evans felt a sense of accomplishment.

Impact on Student Outcomes

As the semester progressed, the impact of these changes became evident. Students who were previously disengaged showed increased participation and interest in the subject matter. Evans implemented formative assessments, allowing him to give timely feedback and adjust his teaching strategies accordingly.

One day, Maria stayed after class. She hesitated for a moment before speaking. "Mr. Roberts, I just wanted to say thank you. I actually enjoy history now. It feels… relevant."

Evans was moved. "Thank you, Maria. That means a lot to me. I'm glad you're finding it interesting."

The shift in his students' attitudes and academic performance was undeniable. Test scores improved, but more importantly, the students were more engaged and motivated. They were not just memorizing facts; they were understanding concepts and developing critical thinking skills.

A Broader Impact

Evans's success did not go unnoticed. His colleagues began to inquire about the changes in his classroom. Encouraged, Evans proposed a series of professional development workshops focused on educational psychology principles.

"Teachers, we need to bridge the gap between theory and practice," he urged during the first workshop. "Understanding our students' cognitive and emotional needs can transform our teaching methods and, ultimately, their learning outcomes."

As the workshops progressed, more teachers embraced the concepts, leading to a school-wide shift in teaching practices. Crestwood High became a model for incorporating educational psychology into everyday teaching, setting a new standard for student engagement and success.

Reflection

In the quiet moments after school, Evans often reflected on his journey. The initial frustration and disillusionment had given way to a profound sense of purpose. By embracing the principles of educational psychology, he had not only revitalized his teaching but also made a significant impact on his students' lives.

He thought back to Maria's question on that fateful day: "Does it even matter?" Now, with a sense of fulfillment, Evans knew the answer. Yes, it mattered immensely. Through understanding and applying educational psychology, he had found a way to make history—and learning itself—matter to his students.

Current Trends and Future Directions

Technological Advancements

Evans Roberts sat in his classroom, the late afternoon sun casting long shadows across the desks. He scrolled through his laptop, reading articles on the latest educational technologies. The seminar on educational psychology had opened his eyes to the myriad ways technology could enhance learning.

Determined to stay ahead, Evans decided to experiment with some of these tools. He began with a simple but effective method: incorporating interactive digital platforms. He introduced his students to a collaborative online tool where they could work on group projects in real time, even from home.

One day, Evans watched as his students engaged in a lively online debate about the ethical implications of industrialization, using the platform to share articles, videos, and comments. Maria, who had previously been disengaged, was one of the most active participants. She created a compelling presentation that compared the environmental impacts of the Industrial Revolution to today's climate crisis, complete with multimedia elements.

"Technology isn't just a tool," Evans thought, watching his students thrive. "It's a bridge that connects theoretical knowledge with practical application, making learning more dynamic and engaging."

Inclusive Education

Inspired by his success with technology, Evans turned his focus to inclusivity. He attended workshops on inclusive education and learned about Universal Design for Learning (UDL), a framework that accommodates all learners regardless of their abilities or backgrounds.

Evans began to adapt his teaching methods to ensure that every student could access the curriculum. He used varied instructional methods, including visual aids, audio recordings, and hands-on activities, to cater to different learning styles.

One notable success was with Jamie, a student with dyslexia who had struggled to keep up with reading-heavy assignments. Evans provided Jamie with audiobooks and speech-to-text software, which allowed him to participate fully in class discussions and complete his assignments on time.

The changes extended beyond academic accommodations. Evans fostered a classroom culture of respect and understanding, where diversity was celebrated, and every student felt valued. He arranged group activities that required collaboration and empathy, helping students learn from each other's perspectives.

During a class project on civil rights movements, students worked in diverse groups, each bringing unique insights and backgrounds to the discussion. Jamie's group produced a powerful presentation on the intersectionality of the civil rights movement, weaving in personal stories that resonated deeply with their peers.

Future Research Areas

Evans's transformation sparked a deep interest in the future of educational psychology. He stayed current with the latest research, attending conferences and reading academic journals. He was particularly intrigued by emerging areas of study, such as the impact of neuroscience on education, the role of emotional intelligence in learning, and the potential of artificial intelligence to personalize education.

One evening, Evans attended a lecture by Dr. Amy Patel, a leading researcher in the field. She spoke about the promising intersections between neuroscience and education, discussing how understanding brain development could revolutionize teaching strategies.

"Imagine a classroom where lessons are tailored to the neural development of each student," Dr. Patel said. "Where cognitive and emotional readiness are considered alongside academic content."

Evans was captivated. He envisioned a future where education was deeply personalized, where teachers used brain-based strategies to optimize learning for every student.

Inspired, he began a small research project with his students, exploring how different learning environments affected their cognitive and emotional engagement. He experimented with flexible seating, sensory tools, and mindfulness exercises, collecting data on their impact.

The results were promising. Students reported feeling more focused and less stressed, and their academic performance improved. Evans shared his findings at a district meeting, advocating for a more research-driven approach to education.

Looking Ahead

Evans's journey was far from over. He knew that staying effective as an educator meant continually evolving, staying informed about new research, and being willing to adapt. The principles of educational psychology had become his compass, guiding him through the ever-changing landscape of education.

In his classroom, the walls were now adorned with student projects, reflecting a diversity of thought and creativity. The room buzzed with energy as students engaged with technology, collaborated on inclusive projects, and explored new ideas.

Evans looked around, filled with a renewed sense of purpose. He had come a long way from the disillusioned teacher who once questioned his methods. Now, he was a pioneer, embracing current trends and future directions in education, always striving to bridge the gap between theory and practice.

As the school bell rang, signaling the end of another day, Evans packed his bag with a sense of accomplishment. He was not just teaching history; he was making history by shaping the future of education, one student at a time.

2

Chapter 2: Cognitive Development and Learning

Theories of Cognitive Development

Piaget's Stages of Development

Evans Roberts stood at the front of his classroom, chalk in hand, feeling a renewed sense of purpose. His students sat in their usual spots, but there was an air of curiosity about them. Today, Evans planned to incorporate Jean Piaget's stages of cognitive development into his teaching.

"Alright, class, today we're going to learn about the Industrial Revolution through a new lens," Evans began. "But first, let's talk about how we learn and develop over time."

He sketched a simple diagram on the board, outlining Piaget's four stages: Sensorimotor, Preoperational, Concrete Operational, and Formal Operational.

"Piaget believed that we go through these stages as we grow," Evans explained. "Each stage represents a different way of thinking and understanding the world."

He divided the class into groups, assigning each a different stage of development to research and present. The students eagerly got to work, using the classroom tablets to gather information.

As they presented, Evans noticed how their understanding deepened. The group studying the Concrete Operational stage discussed how children in this stage begin to think logically about concrete events. They related it to how they first learned to categorize and understand historical events in earlier grades.

Maria, who had taken on the Formal Operational stage, confidently explained, "In this stage, we can think abstractly and use hypothetical reasoning. This is why we're able to understand complex concepts like the impact of industrialization on society."

Evans felt a sense of pride. By engaging with Piaget's theory, his students were not only learning about cognitive development but also seeing how it applied to their own learning processes.

Vygotsky's Sociocultural Theory

The next week, Evans introduced Lev Vygotsky's sociocultural theory. He began the lesson by sharing a personal story about his own learning experiences, emphasizing the importance of social interactions and cultural context.

"Vygotsky believed that our cognitive development is largely influenced by the people around us and the culture we're part of," Evans explained. "He introduced the concept of the Zone of Proximal Development, or ZPD, which is the gap between what a learner can do independently and what they can do with guidance."

He then arranged a peer mentoring activity. Each student was paired with a partner of different skill levels. The task was to solve a series of historical problems related to the Industrial Revolution, requiring them to rely on each other's strengths and knowledge.

Evans walked around the room, observing the interactions. He saw Jamie, usually hesitant to participate, confidently guiding his partner through a difficult concept. In another corner, Maria was patiently explaining the economic impacts of the era to her peer.

"This is amazing," Evans thought. "They're learning from each other, just as Vygotsky suggested."

By the end of the class, the students had not only solved the problems but had also developed a stronger sense of collaboration and mutual respect. Evans realized the power of social learning and the importance of creating a supportive learning community.

Information Processing Theory

Finally, Evans turned his attention to the Information Processing Theory. He began the lesson with a hands-on activity. He handed out index cards with various facts about the Industrial Revolution and asked the students to sort them into categories: innovations, social changes, economic impacts, and so on.

"Think of your brain like a computer," Evans said. "Information comes in, it's processed, and then stored. The way we organize and store information affects how well we can recall it later."

He explained the key components of the Information Processing Theory: encoding, storage, and retrieval. The students were fascinated by the analogy and eagerly participated in the sorting activity.

Next, Evans introduced a memory game to reinforce the concept. He flashed images and key terms on the screen, then asked students to recall and write down as many as they could remember.

As they shared their results, Evans pointed out how organizing information into meaningful categories helped improve recall. He also discussed strategies like chunking and rehearsal, encouraging students to use these techniques in their studies.

"By understanding how our brains process information, we can become more effective learners," Evans concluded. "It's not just about memorizing facts but about making connections and organizing knowledge in a way that makes it easier to retrieve."

Applying the Theories

Evans felt a deep sense of fulfillment. Integrating these cognitive development theories had transformed his classroom. His students were more engaged, their critical thinking skills were improving, and they were making connections between theory and practice.

In a reflective journal entry that evening, Evans wrote, "Today was a breakthrough. By understanding Piaget, Vygotsky, and the Information Processing Theory, I've found new ways to reach my students. It's incredible to see them not just learn, but truly understand and apply these concepts."

The journey was ongoing, but Evans was more confident than ever that he was on the right path. Educational psychology had given him the tools to unlock his students' potential, bridging the gap between theory and practice in a meaningful way.

As he closed his journal, Evans felt a renewed sense of purpose. He was not just teaching history; he was shaping minds and empowering his students to become lifelong learners.

Learning Processes

Memory and Recall

Evans Roberts stood before his class, ready to explore the intricacies of memory and recall with his students. He held up a small box filled with assorted objects: a miniature globe, a feather, a vintage key, and other trinkets. His students watched curiously.

"Today, we're going to dive into how our memory works and how we can improve our recall abilities," Evans announced. He placed the objects on a table and gave the students a minute to observe them.

After collecting the items, he asked, "Now, who can remember all the objects they just saw?"

Hands shot up, and students eagerly began listing the items. Evans noted their responses on the board, highlighting how some students remembered more items than others.

"Memory is a fascinating process," Evans explained. "It involves encoding, storing, and retrieving information. Let's break it down."

He used the example of the objects to explain the different types of memory: sensory memory (the initial perception of the objects), short-term memory (the brief holding of the items in their minds), and long-term memory (where information is stored for extended periods).

To reinforce the lesson, Evans introduced mnemonic devices, such as acronyms and visual imagery, to help the students enhance their memory. They practiced by creating mnemonic phrases for key historical events, like the causes of the Industrial Revolution.

By the end of the lesson, the students were not only able to recall more information but also understood the underlying processes that made memory and recall work.

Problem-Solving Strategies

The next day, Evans decided to tackle problem-solving strategies. He began with a challenging question related to their history lesson: "How could the working conditions during the Industrial Revolution have been improved?"

He divided the class into small groups, each tasked with brainstorming solutions. Evans walked around, listening to their discussions. Some groups focused on reducing work hours, while others suggested better safety regulations or fair wages.

After the brainstorming session, Evans introduced the concept of problem-solving strategies. "There are several steps we can follow to solve problems effectively," he said, writing them on the board: Identify the problem, generate possible solutions, evaluate the options, and implement the best solution.

He guided the students through each step, using their ideas about improving working conditions as a practical example. The class discussed the feasibility of each solution and the potential obstacles they might face.

One group suggested forming a labor union, which led to a lively debate about the pros and cons of collective bargaining.

Maria pointed out historical examples of successful unions, while Jamie highlighted the challenges they faced.

Evans was impressed by their critical thinking and collaborative efforts. By the end of the lesson, the students had developed a deeper understanding of problem-solving and could apply these strategies to various scenarios, both historical and contemporary.

Metacognition

To wrap up the week, Evans introduced the concept of metacognition, or thinking about one's own thinking. He began the lesson with a reflective exercise.

"Take a few minutes to think about how you learn best," Evans instructed. "What strategies do you use to remember information? How do you approach difficult problems?"

The students wrote their thoughts in their journals. Evans then shared his own experiences with metacognition, explaining how being aware of his learning processes had helped him become a more effective teacher.

"Metacognition involves planning, monitoring, and evaluating your learning," Evans said. "It's about being mindful of the strategies you use and understanding what works best for you."

He introduced a self-regulation checklist, which included questions like: Did I understand the lesson? What strategies did I use? What can I do differently next time? The students used the checklist to reflect on their recent projects and assignments.

Evans also encouraged them to set specific learning goals and develop action plans to achieve them. He emphasized the importance of self-assessment and adjusting strategies based on their progress.

Maria, who had become increasingly engaged, shared her thoughts. "I've realized that I learn better when I study in a quiet place and take breaks to review what I've learned. I'm going to try setting aside specific times for study and reflection."

Jamie added, "I think discussing topics with classmates helps me understand better. I'll try to participate more in group studies."

Evans felt a sense of pride as he watched his students take ownership of their learning processes. By understanding and applying metacognitive strategies, they were becoming more self-directed and effective learners.

Empowering Students

As Evans reflected on the week's lessons, he felt a deep sense of accomplishment. He had successfully introduced his students to key cognitive development theories and learning processes, equipping them with valuable tools to enhance their learning.

His students were not only gaining knowledge but also developing critical thinking skills and self-awareness. By understanding how memory, problem-solving, and metacognition worked, they were becoming more independent and confident learners.

Evans knew that this was just the beginning. There was still much to explore in the realm of educational psychology. But for now, he was content knowing that he had made a significant impact on his students' lives.

As the school bell rang, signaling the end of the day, Evans packed his bag with a smile. He was not just teaching history; he was shaping minds, empowering his students to become lifelong learners, and bridging the gap between theory and practice.

Applications in the Classroom

Age-Appropriate Learning Activities

Evans Roberts stood before his class, a stack of colorful materials spread out on his desk. Today, he planned to put theory into practice by designing age-appropriate learning activities that catered to his students' cognitive development.

"Good morning, class!" Evans greeted with enthusiasm. "Today, we're going to embark on an exciting adventure through history using interactive learning activities."

He divided the class into small groups and assigned each group a historical period to explore: Ancient Civilizations, the Middle Ages, the Renaissance, and the Industrial Revolution.

"For each period," Evans explained, "you will create a timeline using the materials provided. Be creative! Use images, symbols, and captions to represent key events and developments."

The students eagerly dove into the task, cutting and pasting their way through history. Evans circulated among the groups, offering guidance and encouragement.

Maria's group, tasked with the Renaissance, meticulously arranged images of famous artworks, inventors, and discoveries on their timeline. Jamie's group, focusing on the Industrial Revolution, used bold colors and symbols to depict the rise of factories and the impact on society.

As the timelines took shape, Evans marveled at the students' creativity and engagement. By tailoring the activity to their cognitive abilities and interests, he had created a dynamic learning experience that brought history to life.

Scaffolding Techniques

The following week, Evans introduced scaffolding techniques to support his students' learning. He began the lesson with a challenging reading passage about the scientific innovations of the Renaissance.

"Today, we're going to use scaffolding to help us understand complex texts," Evans announced. He projected the passage on the board and explained the purpose of scaffolding: providing temporary support to bridge the gap between what students already know and what they need to learn.

He modeled the process by reading the passage aloud, pausing to ask comprehension questions and highlighting key vocabulary. Then, he guided the students through a series of scaffolded activities, such as summarizing the main ideas, identifying unfamiliar words, and making connections to prior knowledge.

As they worked through the activities together, Evans gradually released control, allowing the students to apply the scaffolding techniques independently. Maria, who struggled with reading comprehension, eagerly participated, using the strategies to decode unfamiliar words and infer meaning from context.

By the end of the lesson, the students felt more confident in their ability to tackle challenging texts. Evans had provided them with the support they needed to succeed, building their cognitive skills and fostering independence.

Enhancing Cognitive Skills

In the final part of the chapter, Evans focused on enhancing his students' cognitive skills through interactive exercises and games. He began with a review of key concepts from previous lessons, using a multimedia presentation to engage the students' visual and auditory senses.

Next, he introduced a series of cognitive skills challenges, designed to stretch their thinking and problem-solving abilities. The challenges ranged from puzzles and riddles to logic games and creative brainstorming activities.

The students enthusiastically embraced the challenges, working together to solve problems and overcome obstacles. Evans encouraged them to think critically, consider multiple perspectives, and apply their knowledge in new and creative ways.

Maria's group tackled a logic puzzle that required them to use deductive reasoning to solve a mystery. Jamie's group collaborated on a creative writing task, imagining themselves as historical figures and writing journal entries from their perspectives.

As the class buzzed with excitement, Evans marveled at the transformation in his students. By providing them with opportunities to practice and develop their cognitive skills, he was empowering them to become confident, independent learners.

Empowering Minds

As Evans reflected on the chapter, he felt a deep sense of satisfaction. By applying cognitive development theories and learning processes in the classroom, he had created engaging and effective learning experiences for his students.

His students were not just learning history; they were developing critical thinking skills, problem-solving abilities, and a love of learning that would serve them well in the years to come.

As the school day drew to a close, Evans looked out at his class with pride. He was not just teaching history; he was shaping minds, empowering his students to reach their full potential, and bridging the gap between theory and practice.

With a smile, Evans packed up his materials, already looking forward to the next chapter in their educational journey.

3

Chapter 3: Motivation in Education

Theories of Motivation

Maslow's Hierarchy of Needs

Evans Roberts stood at the front of his classroom, the whiteboard behind him filled with colorful diagrams and notes. Today, he was particularly animated, knowing that understanding motivation was key to unlocking his students' potential.

"Class," Evans began, his voice vibrant with enthusiasm, "today we delve into the fascinating world of motivation theories. Let's start with one of the most well-known: Maslow's Hierarchy of Needs."

He drew a pyramid on the board, labeling each level from the bottom up: physiological needs, safety needs, love and belonging, esteem, and self-actualization.

"Imagine this pyramid represents the journey of human motivation," Evans explained. "Maslow believed that before we can focus on higher-order goals, we must first satisfy our basic needs. For instance, how can a student concentrate on learning if they're hungry or unsafe?"

He walked over to his desk and picked up a small box of granola bars. "This is why schools provide breakfast programs. Meeting physiological needs is the foundation. From there, safety, belonging, and esteem are crucial for students to reach their full potential, their self-actualization."

He paused, letting the concept sink in. "Think about your own experiences. When have you felt most motivated to achieve? What needs were being met?"

The students buzzed with discussion, reflecting on their own hierarchies of needs.

Self-Determination Theory

Evans moved back to the whiteboard, erasing the pyramid and drawing three interconnected circles. "Next, let's talk about Self-Determination Theory, or SDT, developed by Deci and Ryan. This theory focuses on three fundamental needs: autonomy, competence, and relatedness."

He wrote each term in a circle. "Autonomy means having control over your own actions. Competence is feeling effective and capable in what you do. Relatedness is the sense of connection to others."

He pointed to the circles, linking them together with arrows. "When these needs are met, people are intrinsically motivated. They do things because they find them interesting and satisfying, not because of external rewards."

Evans handed out a short survey to the students, asking them to reflect on activities they were intrinsically motivated to do.

"Think about times when you felt truly engaged and motivated. How did these needs play a role?"

The students diligently filled out their surveys, some nodding as they realized the connections between their motivations and SDT.

Expectancy-Value Theory

Finally, Evans turned back to the board and drew a simple equation: Motivation = Expectancy × Value.

"Lastly, we have the Expectancy-Value Theory," he announced. "This theory, developed by Eccles and Wigfield, suggests that motivation is determined by two main factors: expectancy and value."

He wrote 'Expectancy' and 'Value' on the board, drawing a multiplication sign between them. "Expectancy is the belief that one can succeed at a task. Value is the importance or benefit of succeeding at that task."

Evans glanced around the room, his eyes twinkling with curiosity. "Think about a subject you excel in. Why are you motivated to do well in it? Is it because you believe you can succeed, or because you value the outcomes of doing well?"

He gave an example from his own life. "When I was in college, I struggled with mathematics at first. My expectancy was low—I didn't believe I could succeed. But then a great teacher helped me see that with effort, I could improve. My expectancy increased, and so did my motivation."

Evans walked around the room, listening to students share their experiences. Some talked about sports, others about academic subjects, and many realized how their beliefs about their abilities and the value they placed on tasks influenced their motivation.

Empowering Student Motivation

As the lesson on motivation theories concluded, Evans felt a sense of fulfillment. By exploring Maslow's Hierarchy of Needs, Self-Determination Theory, and Expectancy-Value Theory, he had provided his students with valuable insights into what drives their behavior and learning.

His students left the classroom with a deeper understanding of their own motivations and a toolkit of concepts they could apply to enhance their engagement and success. As Evans watched them go, he knew that he was not just teaching history; he was empowering his students to harness the power of motivation in their educational journeys.

With a sense of excitement, Evans looked forward to seeing how these newfound understandings would impact his students' attitudes and achievements in the days and weeks to come.

Intrinsic vs. Extrinsic Motivation

Definitions and Differences

Evans Roberts paced the front of his classroom, a topic of great importance on his mind: intrinsic and extrinsic motivation. He glanced at the clock, knowing the significance of this lesson in shaping his students' approach to learning.

"Today, we're diving into the fascinating world of motivation," Evans began, his voice infused with energy. "We'll explore the differences between intrinsic and extrinsic motivation and how they impact our learning journey."

He drew a simple diagram on the board, contrasting the two types of motivation. "Intrinsic motivation," he explained, "comes from within. It's when we're driven by personal enjoyment, curiosity, or a sense of accomplishment. Extrinsic motivation, on the other hand, comes from external factors like rewards, praise, or avoiding punishment."

Maria raised her hand. "So, intrinsic motivation is when we do something because we want to, and extrinsic motivation is when we do it for a reward or to avoid punishment?"

"Exactly!" Evans replied, impressed by her grasp of the concept. "Now, let's explore how these motivations affect our learning."

Impact on Learning

Evans guided the class through a discussion on the effects of intrinsic and extrinsic motivation on learning. He shared examples of how intrinsic motivation fosters deep engagement and a genuine desire to learn, while extrinsic motivation often leads to short-term compliance but may undermine long-term interest and intrinsic motivation.

"To illustrate," Evans said, "think about a time when you pursued a hobby or interest simply because it brought you joy. That's intrinsic motivation at work. On the other hand, consider a task you completed solely to earn a reward or avoid punishment. That's extrinsic motivation."

The students nodded, recognizing the distinction. Jamie shared his experience with studying for exams, admitting that he often felt more motivated when he was genuinely interested in the subject matter rather than solely focused on grades.

Evans smiled, proud of his students' insights. "By understanding the differences between intrinsic and extrinsic motivation, we can make informed choices about how we approach our learning and foster a love of learning that lasts a lifetime."

Strategies to Foster Intrinsic Motivation

As the discussion progressed, Evans shifted the focus to strategies for fostering intrinsic motivation in the classroom. He emphasized the importance of creating a supportive and engaging learning environment where students feel valued, challenged, and empowered.

"We can cultivate intrinsic motivation by providing opportunities for choice, autonomy, and meaningful learning experiences," Evans explained. "We can tap into students' interests and passions, allowing them to explore topics that resonate with them personally."

He shared examples of classroom activities that promote intrinsic motivation, such as project-based learning, inquiry-based investigations, and student-led discussions. He also highlighted the role of feedback and encouragement in fostering a growth mindset and intrinsic motivation.

"To truly inspire our students, we must tap into their innate curiosity and desire to learn," Evans concluded. "By fostering intrinsic motivation, we empower them to become self-directed, lifelong learners who are motivated by a love of learning itself."

Empowering Learners

As Evans concluded the lesson, he felt a sense of fulfillment. By exploring the concepts of intrinsic and extrinsic motivation, he had equipped his students with valuable insights into their own motivations and learning preferences.

His students left the classroom with a newfound appreciation for the power of intrinsic motivation and a commitment to nurturing their own love of learning. As Evans watched them go, he knew that he was not just teaching history; he was empowering his students to take ownership of their education and pursue their passions with purpose and enthusiasm.

With a smile, Evans looked forward to the next chapter in their educational journey, knowing that his students were well-equipped to navigate the challenges and opportunities that lay ahead.

Classroom Applications

Motivational Teaching Practices

Evans Roberts stood before his class, eager to implement the principles of intrinsic motivation into his teaching practices. He had spent hours preparing engaging activities and fostering a classroom environment that encouraged curiosity and exploration.

"Today, we're going to experience the power of motivational teaching practices firsthand," Evans announced, a spark of excitement in his eyes. "We'll explore ways to ignite your intrinsic motivation and fuel your passion for learning."

He began the lesson with an interactive activity, inviting

students to share their interests and hobbies. The classroom buzzed with energy as students discussed their passions, from music and art to sports and science.

Evans listened intently, taking notes and nodding in encouragement. He made mental connections between their interests and the curriculum, eager to incorporate their passions into future lessons.

"By tapping into your interests and passions," Evans explained, "we can make learning more meaningful and engaging. Let's explore how we can apply this concept to our classroom activities."

Goal Setting and Achievement

Next, Evans introduced the concept of goal setting as a powerful motivator for achievement. He encouraged students to reflect on their academic and personal goals, emphasizing the importance of setting specific, measurable, achievable, relevant, and time-bound (SMART) goals.

"Setting goals gives us direction and purpose," Evans explained. "It helps us stay focused and motivated, even when faced with challenges."

He guided the class through a goal-setting exercise, asking each student to identify a goal they wanted to achieve by the end of the semester. They wrote their goals on colorful sticky notes and placed them on a bulletin board, creating a visual representation of their aspirations.

"Now that we have our goals," Evans said with a smile, "let's work together to support each other and celebrate our achievements along the way."

Creating a Motivating Learning Environment

As the lesson drew to a close, Evans focused on creating a motivating learning environment that nurtured intrinsic motivation. He rearranged the classroom furniture, creating flexible seating arrangements that encouraged collaboration and creativity.

"Your learning environment plays a crucial role in shaping your motivation and engagement," Evans explained. "Let's design a space that inspires curiosity, fosters collaboration, and celebrates diversity."

He invited students to personalize their learning spaces, adding artwork, inspirational quotes, and motivational posters. They rearranged desks, bean bags, and reading nooks, transforming the classroom into a vibrant and welcoming space.

"As we embark on this journey of learning together," Evans said, "let's remember that our classroom is more than just four walls. It's a community of learners, united by a shared passion for knowledge and discovery."

Empowering Growth

As Evans surveyed the transformed classroom, he felt a sense of pride and excitement. By applying motivational teaching practices, goal setting, and creating a motivating learning environment, he had laid the foundation for a successful and fulfilling academic year.

His students left the classroom with a renewed sense of purpose and determination, eager to pursue their goals and explore their interests with passion and enthusiasm. As Evans watched them go, he knew that he was not just teaching history;

he was empowering his students to reach their full potential and become lifelong learners.

With a sense of anticipation, Evans looked forward to the adventures that lay ahead, knowing that together, they would overcome challenges, celebrate achievements, and grow as individuals and as a community of learners.

4

Chapter 4: Classroom Management and Discipline

Exploring Theories and Models

Behaviorist Approaches

Evans Roberts stepped into his classroom, ready to delve into the theories and models of classroom management and discipline. With a stack of textbooks and research papers in hand, he was eager to explore the various approaches that could help him maintain a positive learning environment.

"Good morning, class," Evans greeted, projecting enthusiasm despite the weighty topic at hand. "Today, we're going to embark on a journey through the theories and models of classroom management and discipline."

He began with behaviorist approaches, explaining the fundamental principles of behaviorism and its application in the classroom. Evans discussed how behaviorists focus on observable behaviors and external stimuli, using reinforcement and punishment to shape student conduct.

"As behaviorists," Evans explained, "we aim to reinforce desirable behaviors and discourage undesirable behaviors through a system of rewards and consequences."

He shared examples of behaviorist techniques, such as positive reinforcement, where students receive rewards for demonstrating desired behaviors, and negative reinforcement, where undesired behaviors result in consequences.

As the class engaged in a lively discussion, Evans emphasized the importance of consistency and clear expectations in implementing behaviorist approaches effectively. He outlined strategies for creating a structured and predictable learning environment that promotes positive behavior and minimizes disruptions.

Cognitive-Behavioral Approaches

Transitioning to cognitive-behavioral approaches, Evans introduced the concept of cognitive restructuring and its role in shaping student behavior. He explained how cognitive-behavioral theorists focus on the interplay between thoughts, feelings, and behaviors, aiming to identify and challenge negative thought patterns that contribute to disruptive behavior.

"Cognitive-behavioral approaches encourage students to reflect on their thoughts and emotions," Evans elaborated. "By promoting self-awareness and self-regulation, we can help students develop more adaptive behaviors and coping strategies."

He led the class through a series of cognitive-behavioral exercises, such as identifying and reframing negative thoughts, practicing relaxation techniques to manage stress, and setting achievable goals for behavior change.

As students shared their experiences and insights, Evans emphasized the importance of empathy and understanding in fostering a supportive learning environment. He encouraged students to approach disciplinary issues with compassion and to seek help when needed, emphasizing the value of collaboration and community in promoting positive behavior.

Humanistic Approaches

Finally, Evans turned his attention to humanistic approaches to classroom management and discipline. He discussed the principles of humanism, emphasizing the importance of individual autonomy, self-expression, and intrinsic motivation in fostering positive behavior and academic success.

"As humanists," Evans explained, "we recognize the unique strengths and needs of each student and strive to create a learning environment that respects their dignity and promotes their growth and self-actualization."

He shared examples of humanistic practices, such as student-centered learning, where students take an active role in shaping their educational experiences, and restorative justice, where conflicts are resolved through dialogue and empathy rather than punishment.

Evans highlighted the transformative power of humanistic approaches in building positive relationships between students and teachers, fostering a sense of belonging and empowerment, and cultivating a culture of respect and cooperation in the classroom.

Empowering Relationships

As Evans concluded the lesson, he felt a sense of gratitude for the opportunity to explore the diverse theories and models of classroom management and discipline. By embracing behaviorist, cognitive-behavioral, and humanistic approaches, he had gained valuable insights into the complexities of student behavior and the importance of fostering positive relationships in the classroom.

His students left the classroom with a deeper understanding of the theories and models that underpin effective classroom management and discipline. As Evans watched them go, he knew that he was not just teaching history; he was empowering his students to create inclusive and supportive learning environments where every student can thrive and succeed.

With a renewed sense of purpose, Evans looked forward to applying these theories and models in his own classroom, knowing that together, they would build a community of learners grounded in respect, empathy, and mutual understanding.

Effective Classroom Management Strategies

Establishing Rules and Procedures

Evans Roberts stood at the front of his classroom, ready to delve into the practical strategies of effective classroom management. With a whiteboard marker in hand, he began by outlining the importance of establishing clear rules and procedures.

"Good morning, class," Evans greeted warmly. "Today, we're going to discuss the foundation of a well-managed classroom: rules and procedures."

He engaged the students in a brainstorming session, inviting them to share their ideas on what makes a classroom run smoothly. Together, they compiled a list of expectations for behavior, participation, and academic integrity.

"Rules and procedures provide structure and consistency," Evans explained. "They help us create a safe and orderly learning environment where everyone can focus on their studies."

Using colorful markers, Evans wrote the rules on the board, breaking them down into clear and concise statements. He encouraged students to take ownership of the rules by discussing the rationale behind each one and suggesting revisions or additions.

As the class reviewed the rules together, Evans emphasized the importance of mutual respect and responsibility in upholding them. He encouraged students to hold each other accountable and to contribute to a positive classroom culture where everyone feels valued and respected.

Building Positive Teacher-Student Relationships

Transitioning to the next topic, Evans shifted his focus to the importance of building positive teacher-student relationships. He shared personal anecdotes and examples of how meaningful connections with students can enhance classroom management and foster a supportive learning environment.

"As teachers, our relationships with students are at the heart of effective classroom management," Evans emphasized. "When students feel valued, supported, and understood, they are more likely to engage in learning and follow classroom expectations."

He encouraged students to share their thoughts and feelings, creating opportunities for open dialogue and collaboration. He listened attentively, validating their experiences and perspectives, and offering guidance and encouragement when needed.

Through active listening and empathy, Evans demonstrated his commitment to building authentic connections with his students. He made a conscious effort to learn their names, interests, and strengths, showing genuine interest in their lives both inside and outside the classroom.

Conflict Resolution Techniques

As the lesson drew to a close, Evans addressed the topic of conflict resolution techniques. He emphasized the importance of addressing conflicts promptly and constructively, promoting understanding and reconciliation among students.

"Conflicts are a natural part of classroom life," Evans acknowledged. "But how we respond to them can make all the difference in maintaining a positive learning environment."

He introduced a variety of conflict resolution strategies, such as active listening, perspective-taking, and collaborative problem-solving. He role-played scenarios with the class, demonstrating how to de-escalate tensions and find mutually acceptable solutions.

"By teaching students how to resolve conflicts peacefully," Evans explained, "we empower them to navigate disagreements respectfully and build stronger relationships with their peers."

Empowering a Positive Learning Environment

As Evans concluded the lesson, he felt a sense of fulfillment. By exploring effective classroom management strategies, he had equipped his students with the tools and skills they needed to create a positive learning environment where everyone could thrive.

His students left the classroom with a deeper understanding of the importance of rules and procedures, positive teacher-student relationships, and conflict resolution techniques. As Evans watched them go, he knew that he was not just teaching history; he was empowering his students to build inclusive and supportive communities where everyone feels valued and respected.

With a sense of optimism, Evans looked forward to applying these strategies in his own classroom, knowing that together, they would create a culture of respect, empathy, and cooperation that would enrich the educational experience for all.

Discipline and Behavior Interventions

Positive Behavioral Interventions and Supports (PBIS)

Evans Roberts gathered his students for the next part of their lesson on classroom management and discipline. Today, he planned to introduce them to positive behavioral interventions and supports (PBIS) – an approach aimed at promoting positive behavior and preventing the escalation of challenging behaviors.

"Alright, class," Evans began, his voice carrying a tone of authority and warmth. "Today, we're diving into the world of positive behavioral interventions and supports, or PBIS."

He explained how PBIS focuses on proactive strategies to establish a positive learning environment, emphasizing clear expectations, consistent reinforcement of desired behaviors, and teaching students the skills they need to succeed.

"To implement PBIS effectively," Evans continued, "we must create a school-wide framework that emphasizes respect, responsibility, and resilience."

He engaged the class in a discussion about the core principles of PBIS, encouraging them to brainstorm ways to promote positive behavior in their school community. Together, they identified common expectations for behavior in various settings, such as the classroom, hallways, and cafeteria, and discussed strategies for reinforcing these expectations through praise, incentives, and recognition.

Restorative Practices

Transitioning to the topic of restorative practices, Evans explained how this approach focuses on repairing harm and restoring relationships in the aftermath of conflict or misconduct. He emphasized the importance of empathy, accountability, and dialogue in resolving conflicts and promoting healing.

"As educators," Evans stated, "we have a responsibility to address behavior in a way that promotes growth and reconciliation rather than punishment and exclusion."

He shared examples of restorative practices, such as restorative circles, where students gather to discuss their experiences, express their feelings, and work together to find solutions to conflicts. He emphasized the importance of active listening and respectful communication in creating a safe and supportive environment for dialogue and reflection.

"Restorative practices help us build empathy, understanding, and trust," Evans explained. "By fostering meaningful connections and repairing harm, we can transform conflicts into opportunities for learning and growth."

Individualized Behavior Plans

As the lesson drew to a close, Evans addressed the importance of individualized behavior plans for students with unique behavioral needs. He explained how these plans are tailored to each student's strengths, challenges, and goals, providing targeted support and interventions to address specific behavioral concerns.

"Individualized behavior plans allow us to meet the diverse needs of our students," Evans emphasized. "By collaborating with students, parents, and other support professionals, we can develop strategies to promote positive behavior and academic success."

He encouraged students to reflect on their own behavior and to seek support if they were experiencing challenges. He reassured them that they were not alone and that he was committed to helping them succeed.

Empowering Growth and Accountability

As Evans concluded the lesson, he felt a sense of pride in his students' engagement and understanding. By introducing them to positive behavioral interventions and supports, restorative practices, and individualized behavior plans, he had equipped them with valuable tools and strategies for promoting positive behavior and addressing challenges in the classroom.

His students left the classroom with a deeper understanding of the importance of proactive approaches to discipline and behavior interventions. As Evans watched them go, he knew that he was not just teaching history; he was empowering his students to take ownership of their behavior and to strive for excellence in all areas of their lives.

With a renewed sense of purpose, Evans looked forward to applying these strategies in his own classroom, knowing that together, they would create a culture of respect, empathy, and accountability that would enrich the educational experience for all.

5

Chapter 5: Diversity and Inclusion in Education

Understanding Diversity

Cultural, Ethnic, and Linguistic Diversity

Evans Roberts entered the classroom with a sense of purpose, knowing that today's lesson on diversity and inclusion was crucial for his students' growth and understanding. He began by addressing the rich tapestry of cultural, ethnic, and linguistic diversity that exists within their school community.

"Good morning, class," Evans greeted warmly. "Today, we embark on a journey of exploration and understanding as we delve into the diverse tapestry of our world."

He engaged the class in a discussion about the various cultures, languages, and traditions represented in their school. Students eagerly shared stories of their family backgrounds, customs, and languages spoken at home.

"As we celebrate our differences," Evans emphasized, "we must also recognize the common humanity that unites us all. By embracing diversity, we enrich our learning experiences and cultivate a culture of respect and acceptance."

Socioeconomic Status and Education

Transitioning to the topic of socioeconomic status and education, Evans addressed the impact of economic inequality on students' academic opportunities and outcomes. He explained how factors such as access to quality education, resources, and support services can influence students' success in school.

"As educators," Evans stated, "we have a responsibility to address the systemic barriers that hinder educational equity and social mobility."

He engaged the class in a discussion about the challenges faced by students from low-income families, such as limited access to educational resources, unstable housing, and food insecurity. He emphasized the importance of advocating for policies and programs that promote equity and support students from all socioeconomic backgrounds.

"Every student deserves access to a quality education," Evans declared. "It is our duty to ensure that all students have the support and resources they need to thrive academically and pursue their dreams."

Gender and Sexuality in the Classroom

As the lesson progressed, Evans addressed the topic of gender and sexuality in the classroom, acknowledging the importance of creating an inclusive and supportive environment for all students, regardless of their gender identity or sexual orientation.

"Gender and sexuality are integral aspects of our identities," Evans explained. "It is essential to create a safe and affirming space where all students feel valued and respected for who they are."

He discussed the importance of using inclusive language and materials that reflect the diversity of gender identities and sexual orientations. He encouraged students to challenge stereotypes and discrimination and to promote understanding and acceptance among their peers.

"As educators," Evans stated, "we play a crucial role in fostering a culture of inclusivity and acceptance. By creating a supportive environment where all students feel valued and respected, we empower them to embrace their identities and thrive academically and personally."

Empowering Inclusion

As Evans concluded the lesson, he felt a sense of optimism for the future. By exploring the complexities of cultural, ethnic, and linguistic diversity, socioeconomic status, and gender and sexuality in the classroom, he had equipped his students with the knowledge and empathy needed to navigate the diverse world around them.

His students left the classroom with a deeper understanding of the importance of diversity and inclusion in education. As Evans watched them go, he knew that he was not just teaching history; he was empowering his students to become compassionate and socially responsible citizens who celebrate diversity and advocate for equity and justice in their communities.

With a renewed sense of purpose, Evans looked forward

to continuing the journey of exploration and understanding, knowing that together, they would create a more inclusive and equitable world for future generations.

Inclusive Education Practices

Differentiated Instruction

Evans Roberts continued the discussion on diversity and inclusion by introducing inclusive education practices that cater to the diverse needs of all students in the classroom. He began by explaining the concept of differentiated instruction.

"Good morning, class," Evans greeted with enthusiasm. "Today, we're diving into inclusive education practices that ensure every student can succeed."

He explained how differentiated instruction involves tailoring teaching methods, materials, and assessments to accommodate students' varied learning styles, interests, and abilities.

"As educators," Evans emphasized, "we recognize that every student is unique, with their own strengths, challenges, and preferences. Differentiated instruction allows us to meet students where they are and provide the support and enrichment they need to reach their full potential."

He engaged the class in a discussion about the benefits of differentiated instruction, such as promoting engagement, maximizing learning outcomes, and fostering a sense of belonging and inclusion among all students.

Universal Design for Learning (UDL)

Transitioning to the topic of Universal Design for Learning (UDL), Evans introduced a framework that promotes accessibility and inclusivity by offering multiple means of representation, expression, and engagement.

"UDL ensures that every student has equal access to learning opportunities," Evans explained. "By providing flexible instructional methods and materials, we empower students to demonstrate their knowledge and skills in ways that align with their strengths and preferences."

He shared examples of UDL strategies, such as offering multimedia presentations, providing alternative formats for assignments, and offering choice in how students demonstrate their understanding.

"As we implement UDL principles," Evans stated, "we create a learning environment where all students can thrive, regardless of their background, ability, or learning style."

Culturally Responsive Teaching

As the lesson progressed, Evans addressed the importance of culturally responsive teaching in promoting equity and inclusion in the classroom. He explained how culturally responsive teaching involves recognizing and valuing students' cultural backgrounds, experiences, and perspectives.

"Culturally responsive teaching honors the diversity of our students and integrates their cultural identities into the curriculum," Evans emphasized. "By incorporating diverse perspectives and experiences, we create a more engaging and relevant learning experience for all students."

He shared examples of culturally responsive teaching practices, such as incorporating multicultural literature, integrating culturally relevant examples and materials into lessons, and fostering open dialogue about diverse cultural perspectives.

"As educators," Evans declared, "we have a responsibility to create a classroom environment that celebrates diversity and promotes equity and inclusion. By embracing culturally responsive teaching practices, we empower all students to see themselves reflected in the curriculum and to reach their full potential."

Empowering Inclusion and Equity

As Evans concluded the lesson, he felt a sense of optimism for the future. By exploring inclusive education practices such as differentiated instruction, Universal Design for Learning (UDL), and culturally responsive teaching, he had equipped his students with the tools and strategies needed to create a more inclusive and equitable learning environment.

His students left the classroom with a deeper understanding of the importance of embracing diversity and promoting inclusion in education. As Evans watched them go, he knew that he was not just teaching history; he was empowering his students to become agents of change who advocate for equity and justice in their communities.

With a renewed sense of purpose, Evans looked forward to continuing the journey of promoting diversity, inclusion, and equity in education, knowing that together, they would create a brighter and more inclusive future for all.

Addressing Bias and Discrimination

Implicit Bias in Education

Evans Roberts, with a determined expression, delved into the critical topic of addressing bias and discrimination in education. He knew that acknowledging and confronting implicit bias was essential for creating an inclusive learning environment.

"Class," Evans began, his voice commanding attention, "today, we confront the uncomfortable truth of implicit bias in education."

He explained how implicit bias refers to the unconscious attitudes and stereotypes that influence our perceptions and behaviors, often leading to unintended discrimination against certain groups of students.

"As educators," Evans stressed, "it is our responsibility to recognize and confront our own biases to ensure that all students receive fair and equitable treatment in the classroom."

He engaged the class in a thought-provoking discussion about the ways in which implicit bias manifests in education, from classroom interactions to disciplinary practices. He challenged them to reflect on their own biases and consider how they might impact their interactions with their peers and students.

Anti-Bias Curriculum

Transitioning to the topic of anti-bias curriculum, Evans introduced a framework for addressing bias and promoting diversity, equity, and inclusion in the classroom.

"An anti-bias curriculum," Evans explained, "seeks to challenge stereotypes, promote empathy and understanding, and empower students to become agents of change in their communities."

He shared examples of anti-bias curriculum materials and activities, such as literature that features diverse characters and perspectives, discussions about social justice issues, and projects that encourage students to explore and celebrate their own identities and those of others.

"As educators," Evans declared, "we have the power to shape the hearts and minds of our students. By integrating anti-bias principles into our curriculum, we can cultivate a generation of compassionate and socially conscious individuals who are committed to creating a more just and equitable society."

Promoting Equity and Social Justice

As the lesson progressed, Evans emphasized the importance of promoting equity and social justice in education. He discussed the systemic barriers that perpetuate inequality and outlined strategies for advocating for change at the individual, institutional, and societal levels.

"Promoting equity and social justice requires more than just awareness," Evans stated. "It requires action."

He encouraged students to speak out against injustice, to advocate for marginalized communities, and to work towards creating a more equitable and inclusive world.

"As future leaders and change-makers," Evans concluded, "you have the power to make a difference. Together, we can build a world where every individual is valued, respected, and given the opportunity to thrive."

Empowering Change

As Evans concluded the lesson, he felt a sense of urgency and hope. By addressing bias and discrimination, promoting an anti-bias curriculum, and advocating for equity and social justice, he had equipped his students with the knowledge and skills needed to confront injustice and create positive change in their communities.

His students left the classroom with a renewed sense of purpose and a commitment to challenging bias and discrimination wherever they may encounter it. As Evans watched them go, he knew that he was not just teaching history; he was empowering his students to become courageous advocates for equity and justice in their schools and beyond.

With a sense of determination, Evans looked forward to continuing the journey of promoting diversity, inclusion, and social justice in education, knowing that together, they could create a more equitable and compassionate world for all.

6

Chapter 6: Assessment and Evaluation

Types of Assessments

Formative vs. Summative

Evans Roberts stepped into the classroom, ready to guide his students through the complexities of assessment and evaluation. He began by introducing the distinction between formative and summative assessments, essential components of the educational process.

"Welcome, class," Evans greeted, his voice resonating with enthusiasm. "Today, we embark on a journey to understand the different types of assessments that help us gauge student learning and progress."

He explained how formative assessments are ongoing evaluations used to monitor student understanding and provide feedback for instructional improvement. Meanwhile, summative assessments are administered at the end of a learning period to evaluate student mastery of content and skills.

"As educators," Evans emphasized, "we utilize formative assessments to guide our teaching and support student growth, while summative assessments provide a snapshot of student achievement at a particular point in time."

He engaged the class in a discussion about the benefits of each assessment type, encouraging them to reflect on their own experiences with formative and summative assessments and to consider how they contribute to their learning journey.

Standardized Tests

Transitioning to the topic of standardized tests, Evans addressed their role in educational assessment and evaluation. He explained how standardized tests are designed to measure student performance against a set of predetermined criteria and to provide a standardized measure of achievement across a large population.

"Standardized tests," Evans explained, "offer a way to compare student performance across schools, districts, and even countries. However, they also come with limitations, such as cultural bias and narrow focus on specific subjects."

He engaged the class in a critical discussion about the strengths and weaknesses of standardized tests, encouraging them to consider alternative measures of student achievement that capture a more holistic view of learning.

Alternative Assessments

As the lesson progressed, Evans introduced the concept of alternative assessments as a way to provide more authentic and meaningful measures of student learning. He explained how alternative assessments, such as portfolios, projects, and performance-based assessments, allow students to demonstrate their knowledge and skills in diverse ways.

"Alternative assessments," Evans declared, "offer a more comprehensive view of student learning by allowing students to apply their knowledge and skills in real-world contexts. They also promote creativity, critical thinking, and problem-solving skills."

He shared examples of alternative assessment tasks, such as creating multimedia presentations, conducting research projects, and participating in simulations or debates.

"By incorporating alternative assessments into our practice," Evans stated, "we honor the diverse strengths and talents of our students and provide them with opportunities to showcase their learning in meaningful and authentic ways."

Empowering Growth and Understanding

As Evans concluded the lesson, he felt a sense of satisfaction. By exploring the different types of assessments – formative vs. summative, standardized tests, and alternative assessments – he had equipped his students with a deeper understanding of the complexities of assessment and evaluation in education.

His students left the classroom with a renewed appreciation for the diverse ways in which their learning can be assessed and evaluated. As Evans watched them go, he knew that he was not just teaching history; he was empowering his students to take ownership of their learning and to embrace assessment as a tool for growth and understanding.

With a sense of anticipation, Evans looked forward to continuing the journey of assessment and evaluation with his students, knowing that together, they would navigate the challenges and opportunities that lay ahead.

Principles of Effective Assessment

Validity and Reliability

Evans Roberts continued his exploration of assessment principles, focusing on validity and reliability as essential components of effective assessment practices. He emphasized the importance of ensuring that assessments measure what they intend to measure and produce consistent results over time.

"Welcome back, class," Evans greeted, his tone serious yet engaging. "Today, we delve into the principles of validity and reliability in assessment, vital elements for ensuring the accuracy and fairness of our evaluations."

He explained how validity refers to the extent to which an assessment accurately measures the intended learning outcomes, while reliability pertains to the consistency and stability of assessment results.

"As educators," Evans stated, "we strive to design assessments that are both valid and reliable, providing us with meaningful insights into student learning and progress."

He engaged the class in a discussion about the challenges of ensuring validity and reliability in assessment design, encouraging them to consider strategies for aligning assessments with learning objectives and minimizing sources of measurement error.

Fairness and Bias

Transitioning to the topic of fairness and bias in assessment, Evans addressed the importance of ensuring that assessments are free from bias and discrimination and promote equal opportunities for all students to demonstrate their knowledge and skills.

"Fairness and bias," Evans emphasized, "are critical considerations in assessment design, as they directly impact the validity and equity of our evaluations."

He discussed the various forms of bias that can affect assessment outcomes, such as cultural bias, language bias, and stereotype threat, and explored strategies for mitigating bias and promoting fairness in assessment practices.

"As educators," Evans declared, "we have a responsibility to create assessments that honor the diversity of our students and provide them with equitable opportunities to demonstrate their learning."

Feedback and Improvement

As the lesson progressed, Evans introduced the importance of feedback and improvement in the assessment process. He explained how timely and constructive feedback can support student learning and growth by providing students with clear information about their strengths and areas for improvement.

"Feedback is a powerful tool for learning," Evans stated. "It helps students understand where they stand, identify areas for growth, and set goals for improvement."

He shared examples of effective feedback practices, such as providing specific and actionable feedback, offering opportunities for self-assessment and reflection, and encouraging students to use feedback to guide their learning journey.

"By prioritizing feedback and improvement," Evans concluded, "we empower students to take ownership of their learning and strive for excellence in all areas of their academic and personal development."

Empowering Growth and Excellence

As Evans concluded the lesson, he felt a sense of satisfaction. By exploring the principles of validity and reliability, fairness and bias, and feedback and improvement in assessment, he had equipped his students with the knowledge and skills needed to design and implement effective assessments that support student learning and growth.

His students left the classroom with a deeper understanding of the importance of these principles in assessment design and evaluation. As Evans watched them go, he knew that he was not just teaching history; he was empowering his students to become thoughtful and reflective practitioners who prioritize fairness, equity, and excellence in their assessment practices.

With a sense of optimism, Evans looked forward to continuing the journey of assessment and evaluation with his students, knowing that together, they would create meaningful and impactful learning experiences that inspire growth and success.

Using Assessment Data

Data-Driven Decision Making

Evans Roberts, with a stack of assessment papers in hand, embarked on the next phase of his lesson: using assessment data to inform decision-making. He emphasized the importance of leveraging data to guide instructional practices and support student progress.

"Class," Evans began, his voice filled with determination, "today, we harness the power of assessment data to drive our decision-making and enhance student learning."

He explained how data-driven decision-making involves analyzing assessment results to identify trends, patterns, and areas of strength and improvement. He emphasized the role of assessment data in informing instructional planning, curriculum development, and resource allocation.

"As educators," Evans stated, "we rely on assessment data to guide our instructional practices and ensure that we are meeting the diverse needs of our students."

He engaged the class in a discussion about the benefits of data-driven decision-making, such as identifying students who may need additional support, targeting instruction to address specific learning needs, and measuring the effectiveness of instructional strategies.

Informing Instructional Practices

Transitioning to the topic of informing instructional practices, Evans explored how assessment data can be used to tailor instruction to meet the individual needs of students. He emphasized the importance of using assessment data to differentiate instruction, provide targeted interventions, and scaffold learning experiences.

"Assessment data," Evans explained, "provides us with valuable insights into student understanding, allowing us to adapt our instructional practices to meet students where they are and support their growth and development."

He shared examples of how assessment data can be used to identify students who may benefit from enrichment activities, intervention programs, or personalized learning opportunities.

"By leveraging assessment data," Evans declared, "we can create a learning environment that is responsive to the unique needs and abilities of each student, maximizing their potential for success."

Evaluating Student Progress

As the lesson progressed, Evans addressed the role of assessment data in evaluating student progress over time. He explained how ongoing assessment allows educators to monitor student growth, track achievement trends, and identify areas for improvement.

"Evaluating student progress," Evans stated, "requires us to take a comprehensive view of assessment data, considering both formative and summative assessments, as well as other sources of evidence, such as student work samples and observations."

He engaged the class in a discussion about the importance of communicating assessment results to students and parents, fostering transparency and accountability in the learning process.

"By evaluating student progress," Evans concluded, "we can celebrate achievements, address challenges, and empower students to take ownership of their learning journey."

Empowering Student Success

As Evans concluded the lesson, he felt a sense of fulfillment. By exploring the use of assessment data for data-driven decision-making, informing instructional practices, and evaluating student progress, he had equipped his students with the tools and strategies needed to harness the power of assessment data to support student success.

His students left the classroom with a deeper understanding of the importance of using assessment data to inform their teaching practices and promote student growth and achievement. As Evans watched them go, he knew that he was not just teaching history; he was empowering his students to become reflective and data-informed practitioners who prioritize student success.

With a sense of optimism, Evans looked forward to continuing the journey of using assessment data to drive instructional improvement and promote student learning and growth.

Chapter 7: Instructional Strategies and Methods

Direct Instruction

Lecture Techniques

Evans Roberts, standing at the front of the classroom, prepared to unveil the intricacies of direct instruction. With a confident demeanor, he began by exploring various lecture techniques, a cornerstone of direct instruction.

"Class," Evans announced, his voice projecting with authority, "today, we delve into the art of direct instruction, a powerful method for delivering content in a structured and engaging manner."

He explained how effective lecture techniques involve organizing content logically, delivering information clearly and concisely, and engaging students through active participation and questioning.

"As educators," Evans emphasized, "we strive to captivate our students' attention and facilitate their understanding through dynamic and interactive lectures."

He engaged the class in a demonstration of effective lecture techniques, using visual aids, anecdotes, and real-world examples to bring the content to life. He encouraged students to ask questions and participate in discussions, fostering a collaborative learning environment.

Guided Practice

Transitioning to the topic of guided practice, Evans explored how direct instruction involves providing students with opportunities to apply newly acquired knowledge and skills under the guidance of the teacher.

"Guided practice," Evans explained, "allows students to consolidate their learning through structured activities and exercises that reinforce key concepts and skills."

He shared examples of guided practice activities, such as small group discussions, problem-solving tasks, and hands-on activities, designed to scaffold student learning and promote mastery.

"By providing guided practice," Evans declared, "we empower students to deepen their understanding and develop confidence in their abilities."

Independent Practice

As the lesson progressed, Evans addressed the importance of independent practice in direct instruction. He explained how independent practice allows students to apply their learning autonomously, reinforcing concepts and skills through self-directed activities and assignments.

"Independent practice," Evans stated, "encourages students to take ownership of their learning and develop self-regulation skills that are essential for academic success."

He shared examples of independent practice tasks, such as homework assignments, projects, and research tasks, designed to challenge students and foster independent thinking and problem-solving.

"By providing opportunities for independent practice," Evans concluded, "we empower students to become lifelong learners who are capable of applying their knowledge and skills in diverse contexts."

Empowering Learning

As Evans concluded the lesson on direct instruction, he felt a sense of accomplishment. By exploring lecture techniques, guided practice, and independent practice as components of direct instruction, he had equipped his students with a deeper understanding of effective instructional strategies.

His students left the classroom with a newfound appreciation for the art of direct instruction and a commitment to implementing these strategies in their own teaching practice. As Evans watched them go, he knew that he was not just teaching history; he was empowering his students to become effective and engaging educators who inspire learning and growth in their students.

With a sense of pride, Evans looked forward to witnessing the impact of direct instruction on student learning and achievement in the days and weeks to come.

Constructivist Approaches

Inquiry-Based Learning

Evans Roberts, with a gleam of excitement in his eyes, embarked on the next phase of his lesson: exploring constructivist approaches to instruction. He introduced inquiry-based learning as a method that encourages students to construct their own understanding through exploration and discovery.

"Class," Evans began, his voice filled with enthusiasm, "today, we embark on a journey of inquiry-based learning, where curiosity leads to discovery and understanding."

He explained how inquiry-based learning involves posing questions, conducting investigations, and drawing conclusions, allowing students to actively engage in the learning process and construct meaning from their experiences.

"As educators," Evans emphasized, "we foster a spirit of inquiry and curiosity in our students, empowering them to explore and make sense of the world around them."

He engaged the class in a discussion about the benefits of inquiry-based learning, such as promoting critical thinking, problem-solving skills, and a deeper understanding of content.

Project-Based Learning

Transitioning to the topic of project-based learning, Evans explored how this approach allows students to explore complex topics and real-world problems through hands-on projects and collaborative activities.

"Project-based learning," Evans explained, "challenges students to apply their knowledge and skills to solve authentic problems and create meaningful products."

He shared examples of project-based learning experiences, such as designing a community garden, conducting a scientific investigation, or creating a multimedia presentation, designed to promote creativity, collaboration, and innovation.

"By engaging in project-based learning," Evans declared, "students develop essential 21st-century skills and become active participants in their own learning journey."

Cooperative Learning

As the lesson progressed, Evans addressed the importance of cooperative learning as a constructivist approach to instruction. He explained how cooperative learning involves students working together in small groups to achieve common goals and share their knowledge and expertise.

"Cooperative learning," Evans stated, "fosters collaboration, communication, and teamwork, allowing students to learn from one another and develop a deeper understanding of the content."

He shared examples of cooperative learning activities, such as group projects, peer tutoring, and collaborative problem-solving tasks, designed to promote social interaction and shared responsibility.

"By engaging in cooperative learning," Evans concluded, "students develop empathy, leadership skills, and a sense of community, preparing them for success in an interconnected world."

Empowering Exploration and Collaboration

As Evans concluded the lesson on constructivist approaches, he felt a sense of excitement for the possibilities ahead. By exploring inquiry-based learning, project-based learning, and cooperative learning as methods for fostering student exploration and collaboration, he had equipped his students with the tools and strategies needed to create dynamic and engaging learning experiences.

His students left the classroom inspired to embrace constructivist approaches in their own teaching practice and to empower their students to become active participants in their learning journey. As Evans watched them go, he knew that he was not just teaching history; he was empowering his students to become agents of change who inspire curiosity, creativity, and collaboration in their students.

With a sense of anticipation, Evans looked forward to witnessing the impact of constructivist approaches on student learning and achievement in the days and weeks to come.

This dramatization of Chapter 7 continues Evans's exploration of instructional strategies and methods, focusing on constructivist approaches such as inquiry-based learning, project-based learning, and cooperative learning, highlighting their importance in promoting student exploration, creativity, and collaboration.

Integrating Technology

Digital Tools and Resources

Evans Roberts, with a tablet in hand, embarked on the next phase of his lesson: integrating technology into instructional practices. He introduced a world of digital tools and resources that enhance teaching and learning experiences.

"Class," Evans began, his voice resonating with excitement, "today, we explore the vast possibilities of integrating technology into our instructional practices, unlocking new avenues for engagement and learning."

He explained how digital tools and resources, such as educational apps, multimedia presentations, and interactive simulations, provide opportunities for students to explore concepts in dynamic and immersive ways.

"As educators," Evans emphasized, "we harness the power of technology to enrich our teaching and provide students with access to a wealth of information and resources."

He engaged the class in a demonstration of digital tools, showcasing interactive learning platforms, virtual field trips, and online research databases. He encouraged students to explore these resources and discover their potential for enhancing their learning experiences.

Blended Learning Models

Transitioning to the topic of blended learning models, Evans explored how technology can be seamlessly integrated into traditional classroom settings to create a blended learning environment.

"Blended learning," Evans explained, "combines face-to-face instruction with online learning activities, allowing for greater flexibility, personalization, and differentiation."

He shared examples of blended learning models, such as flipped classrooms, station rotations, and hybrid courses, designed to accommodate diverse learning needs and preferences.

"Blended learning," Evans declared, "empowers students to take control of their learning journey, providing them with opportunities for self-paced learning, collaborative exploration, and personalized instruction."

Online and Remote Instruction

As the lesson progressed, Evans addressed the role of technology in facilitating online and remote instruction, particularly in the context of virtual classrooms and remote learning environments.

"In today's digital age," Evans stated, "technology has become a vital tool for connecting students and educators across distances and providing access to quality education from anywhere, at any time."

He shared examples of online instructional platforms, video conferencing tools, and digital collaboration spaces, designed to facilitate engagement and interaction in virtual learning environments.

"Online and remote instruction," Evans concluded, "allow us to transcend physical boundaries and provide students with the flexibility and accessibility they need to succeed in today's interconnected world."

Empowering Digital Learning

As Evans concluded the lesson on integrating technology, he felt a sense of optimism for the future. By exploring digital tools and resources, blended learning models, and online and remote instruction, he had equipped his students with the knowledge and skills needed to harness the power of technology to enhance teaching and learning experiences.

His students left the classroom inspired to embrace technology in their own instructional practices and to explore innovative ways of engaging their students in digital learning environments. As Evans watched them go, he knew that he was not just teaching history; he was empowering his students to become digital-age educators who embrace technology as a tool for transforming education and empowering learners.

With a sense of excitement, Evans looked forward to witnessing the impact of technology on student learning and achievement in the days and weeks to come.

8

Chapter 8: Social and Emotional Learning (SEL)

Importance of SEL

Emotional Regulation

Evans Roberts, with a warm smile, welcomed his students to the topic of Social and Emotional Learning (SEL). He emphasized the importance of SEL in fostering emotional regulation, the ability to recognize and manage one's emotions effectively.

"Class," Evans began, his tone gentle yet authoritative, "today, we embark on a journey to explore the importance of Social and Emotional Learning, starting with the crucial aspect of emotional regulation."

He explained how emotional regulation allows individuals to identify and cope with their feelings in constructive ways, promoting mental well-being and resilience in the face of challenges.

"As educators," Evans emphasized, "we recognize the significance of equipping our students with the skills to navigate their emotions and regulate their responses to various situations."

He engaged the class in a discussion about strategies for promoting emotional regulation, such as mindfulness practices, breathing exercises, and self-reflection activities. He encouraged students to reflect on their own emotional experiences and consider how they can cultivate a greater sense of emotional awareness and control.

Social Skills Development

Transitioning to the topic of social skills development, Evans highlighted the role of SEL in nurturing interpersonal skills and fostering positive relationships with others.

"Social skills," Evans explained, "are essential for navigating social interactions, collaborating with others, and building healthy relationships."

He shared examples of social skills, such as active listening, empathy, communication, and conflict resolution, and discussed how SEL programs provide opportunities for students to practice and strengthen these skills in various contexts.

"As educators," Evans declared, "we recognize the importance of cultivating a positive and supportive learning environment where students feel valued, respected, and connected to their peers and teachers."

Relationship Building

As the lesson progressed, Evans addressed the importance of relationship building in SEL, emphasizing the role of supportive relationships in promoting social and emotional well-being.

"Relationships," Evans stated, "are the foundation of a healthy school community. They provide students with a sense of belonging, support, and security, essential ingredients for academic and personal success."

He shared examples of strategies for building positive relationships in the classroom, such as fostering a sense of community, promoting inclusivity and acceptance, and providing opportunities for meaningful connections between students and teachers.

"As educators," Evans concluded, "we have the privilege and responsibility to cultivate a culture of kindness, empathy, and respect in our classrooms, where every student feels seen, heard, and valued."

Empowering Social and Emotional Growth

As Evans concluded the lesson on the importance of SEL, he felt a sense of fulfillment. By exploring emotional regulation, social skills development, and relationship building as key components of SEL, he had equipped his students with the knowledge and skills needed to foster social and emotional well-being in themselves and others.

His students left the classroom inspired to prioritize SEL in their own lives and to create supportive and inclusive environments where all individuals can thrive. As Evans watched them go, he knew that he was not just teaching history;

he was empowering his students to become compassionate and empathetic leaders who prioritize the well-being of themselves and others.

With a sense of optimism, Evans looked forward to witnessing the impact of SEL on student growth and development in the days and weeks to come.

Frameworks and Models

CASEL's SEL Framework

Evans Roberts, with a sense of purpose, delved into the various frameworks and models that guide Social and Emotional Learning (SEL) programs. He introduced the Collaborative for Academic, Social, and Emotional Learning (CASEL) framework as a comprehensive guide for promoting SEL in schools.

"Class," Evans began, his voice resonating with conviction, "today, we explore the CASEL framework, a leading model for cultivating social and emotional competencies in students."

He explained how the CASEL framework encompasses five core competencies: self-awareness, self-management, social awareness, relationship skills, and responsible decision-making.

"As educators," Evans emphasized, "we use the CASEL framework to design SEL programs that address the diverse needs of our students and promote their holistic development."

He engaged the class in a discussion about the components of the CASEL framework, encouraging them to consider how each competency contributes to their social and emotional well-being.

Mindfulness Practices

Transitioning to the topic of mindfulness practices, Evans highlighted the role of mindfulness in promoting self-awareness, emotional regulation, and overall well-being.

"Mindfulness," Evans explained, "involves paying attention to the present moment with curiosity and without judgment, allowing individuals to cultivate greater awareness of their thoughts, feelings, and sensations."

He shared examples of mindfulness practices, such as mindful breathing, body scans, and guided meditation, and discussed how these practices can be integrated into daily routines to reduce stress, enhance focus, and improve emotional resilience.

"As educators," Evans declared, "we incorporate mindfulness practices into our classrooms to create a calm and supportive learning environment where students can thrive."

Trauma-Informed Education

As the lesson progressed, Evans addressed the importance of trauma-informed education in promoting SEL, particularly for students who have experienced adversity or trauma.

"Trauma-informed education," Evans stated, "involves creating safe, supportive, and nurturing environments that recognize the impact of trauma on learning and behavior."

He shared strategies for implementing trauma-informed practices in schools, such as building trusting relationships, providing opportunities for self-expression and regulation, and offering trauma-sensitive supports and interventions.

"By adopting a trauma-informed approach," Evans concluded, "we can create a school culture that fosters healing, resilience, and academic success for all students."

Empowering SEL Implementation

As Evans concluded the lesson on frameworks and models for SEL, he felt a sense of determination. By exploring the CASEL framework, mindfulness practices, and trauma-informed education as guiding principles for SEL implementation, he had equipped his students with the knowledge and strategies needed to promote social and emotional well-being in their classrooms and beyond.

His students left the classroom inspired to integrate SEL into their teaching practice and to create nurturing and inclusive environments where all students can thrive. As Evans watched them go, he knew that he was not just teaching history; he was empowering his students to become agents of change who prioritize the social and emotional well-being of themselves and others.

With a sense of hope, Evans looked forward to witnessing the transformative impact of SEL on student lives and school communities in the days and weeks to come.

This dramatization of Chapter 8 continues Evans's exploration of Social and Emotional Learning (SEL), focusing on frameworks and models such as the CASEL framework, mindfulness practices, and trauma-informed education, highlighting their importance in promoting social and emotional well-being in students and creating nurturing and inclusive learning environments.

Classroom Applications

SEL Curriculum Integration

Evans Roberts, now deeply immersed in the topic of Social and Emotional Learning (SEL), transitioned to discussing how SEL principles can be integrated into the classroom curriculum. He emphasized the importance of weaving SEL into every aspect of teaching and learning.

"Class," Evans began, his voice filled with conviction, "now that we understand the foundations of SEL, let's explore how we can integrate these principles into our everyday classroom activities."

He explained how SEL curriculum integration involves infusing social and emotional skills into academic instruction, creating opportunities for students to practice and apply these skills in authentic contexts.

"As educators," Evans emphasized, "we have the power to embed SEL into our lesson plans, activities, and assessments, fostering a holistic approach to student development."

He engaged the class in a discussion about strategies for integrating SEL into various subject areas, such as incorporating discussions on empathy and perspective-taking in language arts, teaching conflict resolution skills during group work in math, and promoting self-awareness through reflective writing in social studies.

Creating a Supportive Classroom Environment

Transitioning to the topic of creating a supportive classroom environment, Evans highlighted the critical role of the classroom climate in promoting social and emotional well-being.

"Our classroom," Evans declared, "is more than just a physical space—it's a community where every student feels valued, respected, and supported."

He shared strategies for creating a positive and inclusive classroom environment, such as establishing clear expectations and routines, promoting kindness and empathy, and providing opportunities for student voice and choice.

"By fostering a supportive classroom environment," Evans stated, "we create a foundation for SEL to flourish, allowing students to feel safe to take risks, express themselves authentically, and collaborate with their peers."

Measuring SEL Outcomes

As the lesson progressed, Evans addressed the importance of measuring SEL outcomes to assess the effectiveness of SEL interventions and programs.

"Measuring SEL outcomes," Evans explained, "allows us to track student progress, identify areas for growth, and make data-informed decisions about our instructional practices."

He shared examples of SEL assessment tools and strategies, such as self-assessments, observation checklists, and student surveys, designed to capture various aspects of social and emotional development.

"By measuring SEL outcomes," Evans concluded, "we can demonstrate the impact of SEL on student learning and well-being, and advocate for continued support and investment in SEL initiatives."

Empowering SEL Implementation

As Evans concluded the lesson on classroom applications of SEL, he felt a sense of fulfillment. By exploring SEL curriculum integration, creating a supportive classroom environment, and measuring SEL outcomes, he had equipped his students with the knowledge and tools needed to promote social and emotional well-being in their classrooms and beyond.

His students left the classroom inspired to infuse SEL into their teaching practice and to create nurturing and inclusive learning environments where all students can thrive. As Evans watched them go, he knew that he was not just teaching history; he was empowering his students to become compassionate and empathetic educators who prioritize the social and emotional well-being of themselves and others.

With a sense of purpose, Evans looked forward to witnessing the transformative impact of SEL on student lives and school communities in the days and weeks to come.

9

Chapter 9: Special Education and Support Services

Understanding Special Education

Definition and Categories

Evans Roberts, with a sense of reverence for inclusivity and diversity, began his exploration of special education and support services. He emphasized the importance of understanding the complexities of special education to provide equitable opportunities for all students.

"Class," Evans began, his voice filled with empathy and respect, "today, we embark on a journey to understand special education and the support services available to students with diverse learning needs."

He explained how special education encompasses a range of services and interventions designed to meet the unique needs of students with disabilities or exceptionalities.

"As educators," Evans emphasized, "we recognize the value of embracing diversity and creating inclusive learning environments where all students can thrive."

He engaged the class in a discussion about the categories of disabilities recognized under special education law, such as learning disabilities, intellectual disabilities, autism spectrum disorders, and emotional or behavioral disorders. He encouraged students to consider the strengths and challenges associated with each disability category and reflect on the implications for teaching and learning.

Legal and Ethical Considerations

Transitioning to the topic of legal and ethical considerations in special education, Evans highlighted the importance of upholding the rights and dignity of students with disabilities.

"Legal and ethical considerations," Evans explained, "guide our practices and decisions in special education, ensuring that we provide students with the support and accommodations they need to access a free and appropriate education."

He discussed key legislation, such as the Individuals with Disabilities Education Act (IDEA) and Section 504 of the Rehabilitation Act, which guarantee students with disabilities the right to a free and appropriate public education and protect them from discrimination based on their disability.

"As educators," Evans declared, "we have a moral and legal obligation to advocate for the rights of students with disabilities and ensure that they receive the support and accommodations they need to succeed."

Individualized Education Programs (IEPs)

As the lesson progressed, Evans addressed the importance of Individualized Education Programs (IEPs) in special education. He explained how IEPs are comprehensive plans developed collaboratively by educators, parents, and other professionals to outline the unique learning goals, accommodations, and services for students with disabilities.

"IEPs," Evans stated, "are tailored to meet the individual needs of each student, providing a roadmap for their educational journey and guiding instruction and support."

He shared examples of components typically included in an IEP, such as present levels of performance, annual goals, special education services, related services, and accommodations or modifications.

"By developing and implementing IEPs," Evans concluded, "we ensure that students with disabilities receive the personalized support they need to achieve their full potential and participate meaningfully in their educational experiences."

Empowering Inclusive Education

As Evans concluded the lesson on understanding special education, he felt a sense of reverence for the importance of inclusivity and equity in education. By exploring the definition and categories of special education, legal and ethical considerations, and the role of Individualized Education Programs (IEPs), he had equipped his students with the knowledge and empathy needed to support students with diverse learning needs.

His students left the classroom inspired to advocate for inclusivity and equity in their own teaching practice and to create supportive and inclusive learning environments where all students can thrive. As Evans watched them go, he knew that he was not just teaching history; he was empowering his students to become compassionate and inclusive educators who prioritize the rights and dignity of all students.

With a sense of purpose, Evans looked forward to witnessing the transformative impact of inclusive education on student lives and school communities in the days and weeks to come.

Supporting Students with Disabilities

Inclusive Classroom Strategies

Evans Roberts, now deeply immersed in the intricacies of special education, transitioned to discussing strategies for supporting students with disabilities in the inclusive classroom. He emphasized the importance of creating environments where all students feel valued, respected, and included.

"Class," Evans began, his voice filled with compassion and determination, "now that we understand the foundations of special education, let's explore how we can support students with disabilities in our inclusive classrooms."

He explained how inclusive classroom strategies involve adapting instruction, materials, and environments to meet the diverse needs of all learners, regardless of ability or disability.

"As educators," Evans emphasized, "we strive to create classrooms where every student feels welcome, supported, and challenged to reach their full potential."

He engaged the class in a discussion about strategies for promoting inclusivity in the classroom, such as differentiated instruction, universal design for learning (UDL), and peer support arrangements. He encouraged students to consider how these strategies can foster a sense of belonging and empower students with disabilities to participate actively in the learning process.

Accommodations and Modifications

Transitioning to the topic of accommodations and modifications, Evans highlighted the importance of providing individualized supports to students with disabilities to ensure their success in the classroom.

"Accommodations and modifications," Evans explained, "are adjustments made to the curriculum, instruction, or environment to address the unique learning needs of students with disabilities."

He shared examples of accommodations and modifications, such as extended time on assessments, preferential seating, alternative assignments, and assistive technology tools, and discussed how these supports can help students access the curriculum and demonstrate their knowledge and skills.

"By providing accommodations and modifications," Evans stated, "we remove barriers to learning and create opportunities for students with disabilities to participate meaningfully in their educational experiences."

Collaboration with Special Education Staff

As the lesson progressed, Evans addressed the importance of collaboration with special education staff in supporting students with disabilities. He emphasized the value of teamwork and shared responsibility in meeting the diverse needs of all learners.

"Collaboration with special education staff," Evans declared, "allows us to leverage our collective expertise and resources to provide comprehensive support to students with disabilities."

He discussed strategies for collaboration, such as co-planning lessons, sharing student progress and concerns, and implementing co-teaching models, and highlighted the benefits of working together to ensure that students receive the support they need to succeed.

"By collaborating with special education staff," Evans concluded, "we create a culture of collaboration and shared responsibility where every student has the opportunity to thrive."

Empowering Inclusive Education

As Evans concluded the lesson on supporting students with disabilities, he felt a sense of determination. By exploring inclusive classroom strategies, accommodations and modifications, and collaboration with special education staff, he had equipped his students with the knowledge and tools needed to create inclusive and supportive learning environments for all students.

His students left the classroom inspired to advocate for inclusivity and equity in their own teaching practice and to collaborate with colleagues to ensure that every student receives the support they need to succeed. As Evans watched them go, he knew that he was not just teaching history; he was empowering his students to become compassionate and inclusive educators who prioritize the success and well-being of all students.

With a sense of hope, Evans looked forward to witnessing the transformative impact of inclusive education on student lives and school communities in the days and weeks to come.

Intervention and Support Services

Response to Intervention (RTI)

Evans Roberts, now delving deeper into the realm of intervention and support services, began to discuss the importance of Response to Intervention (RTI) in meeting the diverse needs of students in the classroom. He emphasized the proactive approach of RTI in identifying and addressing academic and behavioral challenges early on.

"Class," Evans began, his voice filled with determination, "let's explore the concept of Response to Intervention (RTI) and its role in supporting students who may be struggling academically or behaviorally."

He explained how RTI involves a multi-tiered system of support that provides increasingly intensive interventions based on student needs and responsiveness to instruction.

"As educators," Evans emphasized, "we use RTI to identify students who may need additional support, intervene early to address their needs, and monitor their progress over time."

He engaged the class in a discussion about the components of RTI, such as universal screening, progress monitoring, and tiered interventions, and discussed how these components work together to ensure that all students receive the support they need to succeed.

Speech and Language Therapy

Transitioning to the topic of speech and language therapy, Evans highlighted the importance of addressing communication challenges in students with speech and language disorders.

"Speech and language therapy," Evans explained, "is a specialized service that focuses on improving communication skills, such as speaking, listening, and understanding language."

He shared examples of speech and language disorders, such as articulation disorders, language delays, and stuttering, and discussed how speech and language therapists work with students to develop individualized therapy plans tailored to their specific needs.

"As educators," Evans stated, "we collaborate with speech and language therapists to support students with communication challenges and create environments where all students can effectively communicate and participate in learning activities."

Occupational and Physical Therapy

As the lesson progressed, Evans addressed the importance of occupational and physical therapy in supporting students with physical and motor challenges.

"Occupational and physical therapy," Evans declared, "focuses on improving students' ability to participate in everyday activities and develop skills for independence and mobility."

He shared examples of conditions that may require occupational or physical therapy, such as fine motor delays, sensory processing disorders, and physical disabilities, and discussed how therapists work with students to develop customized therapy plans to address their unique needs.

"By providing occupational and physical therapy services," Evans concluded, "we empower students to overcome physical barriers and achieve their full potential in school and beyond."

Empowering Student Success

As Evans concluded the lesson on intervention and support services, he felt a sense of empowerment. By exploring Response to Intervention (RTI), speech and language therapy, and occupational and physical therapy as vital support services for students, he had equipped his students with the knowledge and understanding needed to advocate for the diverse needs of all learners.

His students left the classroom inspired to collaborate with colleagues and support staff to ensure that every student receives the intervention and support services they need to succeed. As Evans watched them go, he knew that he was not just teaching history; he was empowering his students to become advocates for inclusivity and equity in education.

With a sense of determination, Evans looked forward to witnessing the transformative impact of intervention and support services on student lives and school communities in the days and weeks to come.

10

Chapter 10: Professional Development for Educators

Importance of Continuous Learning

Staying Current with Educational Research

Evans Roberts, now shifting his focus to the professional development of educators, began to emphasize the importance of continuous learning in the ever-evolving field of education. He highlighted the significance of staying abreast of current research and best practices to enhance teaching effectiveness and student outcomes.

"Class," Evans began, his voice filled with enthusiasm, "let's delve into the importance of continuous learning for educators and how it contributes to our growth and effectiveness in the classroom."

He explained how staying current with educational research allows educators to access the latest findings and insights in teaching and learning, enabling them to incorporate evidence-based practices into their instructional strategies.

"As educators," Evans emphasized, "we embrace a commitment to lifelong learning, seeking out opportunities to expand our knowledge and refine our teaching practices."

He engaged the class in a discussion about the role of educational research in informing teaching decisions, encouraging them to explore research journals, attend conferences, and participate in professional development workshops to stay informed about emerging trends and innovations in education.

Reflective Teaching Practices

Transitioning to the topic of reflective teaching practices, Evans highlighted the importance of self-reflection and critical inquiry in professional growth and development.

"Reflective teaching," Evans explained, "involves examining our teaching practices, beliefs, and assumptions to identify areas for improvement and refine our approach to instruction."

He shared examples of reflective practices, such as journaling, peer observation, and classroom video analysis, and discussed how these practices can help educators gain insights into their teaching effectiveness and student engagement.

"As educators," Evans stated, "we embrace a culture of reflection and continuous improvement, recognizing that self-awareness and introspection are essential components of professional growth."

CHAPTER 10: PROFESSIONAL DEVELOPMENT FOR EDUCATORS

Professional Learning Communities (PLCs)

As the lesson progressed, Evans addressed the importance of Professional Learning Communities (PLCs) in supporting educators' professional growth and collaboration.

"PLCs," Evans declared, "are collaborative groups of educators who come together to share expertise, resources, and experiences, with the goal of improving teaching and learning outcomes."

He shared examples of PLC activities, such as collaborative lesson planning, data analysis, and instructional rounds, and discussed how PLCs provide opportunities for educators to engage in meaningful dialogue, exchange ideas, and support one another in their professional growth journey.

"By participating in PLCs," Evans concluded, "we foster a culture of collaboration and collective responsibility, where educators work together to ensure the success of every student."

Empowering Professional Growth

As Evans concluded the lesson on professional development for educators, he felt a sense of empowerment. By exploring the importance of continuous learning, reflective teaching practices, and Professional Learning Communities (PLCs) as essential components of professional growth, he had equipped his students with the knowledge and tools needed to cultivate a culture of excellence in education.

His students left the classroom inspired to embrace a commitment to lifelong learning and to seek out opportunities for collaboration and growth in their professional practice. As Evans watched them go, he knew that he was not just teaching history; he was empowering his students to become lifelong learners and leaders in the field of education.

With a sense of optimism, Evans looked forward to witnessing the transformative impact of professional development on educator effectiveness and student achievement in the days and weeks to come.

Effective Professional Development

Workshops and Seminars

Evans Roberts, now delving into effective professional development strategies for educators, emphasized the value of workshops and seminars in fostering continuous learning and skill development. He highlighted the interactive and collaborative nature of these learning experiences, which provide opportunities for educators to engage with new ideas, practices, and colleagues.

"Class," Evans began, his voice brimming with enthusiasm, "let's explore the effectiveness of workshops and seminars as avenues for professional development in education."

He explained how workshops and seminars offer targeted training on specific topics or skills, allowing educators to deepen their understanding and refine their practice in areas of interest or need.

"As educators," Evans emphasized, "we value the opportunity to engage in hands-on learning experiences and collaborate with colleagues to explore new ideas and strategies."

He engaged the class in a discussion about their experiences with workshops and seminars, encouraging them to reflect on the value of interactive learning activities, expert presenta-

Online Courses and Webinars

Transitioning to the topic of online courses and webinars, Evans highlighted the flexibility and accessibility of digital learning platforms in providing professional development opportunities for educators.

"Online courses and webinars," Evans explained, "offer educators the convenience of anytime, anywhere learning, allowing them to access high-quality resources and expertise from the comfort of their own homes."

He shared examples of online courses and webinars available on a wide range of topics, such as instructional strategies, technology integration, and cultural competency, and discussed how these digital learning experiences can accommodate diverse learning preferences and schedules.

"As educators," Evans stated, "we embrace the potential of online learning to expand our knowledge and skills and stay current with emerging trends and innovations in education."

Mentorship and Coaching

As the lesson progressed, Evans addressed the importance of mentorship and coaching in supporting educator growth and development.

"Mentorship and coaching," Evans declared, "provide personalized support and guidance to educators as they navigate their professional journey."

He shared examples of mentorship and coaching programs,

such as peer mentoring, instructional coaching, and leadership mentoring, and discussed how these relationships can offer valuable feedback, encouragement, and accountability to educators seeking to improve their practice.

"By engaging in mentorship and coaching," Evans concluded, "we cultivate a culture of collaboration and continuous improvement, where educators support one another in their quest for excellence."

Empowering Professional Growth

As Evans concluded the lesson on effective professional development, he felt a sense of empowerment. By exploring workshops and seminars, online courses and webinars, and mentorship and coaching as effective strategies for educator growth and development, he had equipped his students with the knowledge and resources needed to pursue lifelong learning and excellence in their professional practice.

His students left the classroom inspired to embrace a variety of professional development opportunities and to cultivate a culture of collaboration and continuous improvement in their schools and communities. As Evans watched them go, he knew that he was not just teaching history; he was empowering his students to become lifelong learners and leaders in the field of education.

With a sense of optimism, Evans looked forward to witnessing the transformative impact of effective professional development on educator effectiveness and student achievement in the days and weeks to come.

Implementing Change in the Classroom

Adapting New Strategies

Evans Roberts, now transitioning to the practical application of professional development, emphasized the importance of implementing change in the classroom. He highlighted the need for educators to adapt new strategies and practices learned through professional development experiences to meet the diverse needs of their students.

"Class," Evans began, his voice filled with encouragement, "let's explore the process of implementing change in the classroom and how it contributes to our growth as educators."

He explained how implementing change involves adopting new strategies and practices that align with the goals and objectives of professional development initiatives.

"As educators," Evans emphasized, "we embrace a growth mindset, continually seeking opportunities to refine our practice and enhance student learning."

He engaged the class in a discussion about strategies for adapting new strategies in the classroom, encouraging them to reflect on their teaching practice and consider how they can incorporate innovative approaches to meet the needs of their students.

Evaluating Effectiveness

Transitioning to the topic of evaluating effectiveness, Evans highlighted the importance of monitoring and assessing the impact of new strategies and practices on student learning outcomes.

"Evaluating effectiveness," Evans explained, "allows us to determine whether the changes we implement in the classroom are achieving the desired results and making a positive difference in student learning."

He shared examples of assessment tools and strategies, such as student surveys, classroom observations, and formative assessments, and discussed how these measures can provide valuable feedback on the effectiveness of instructional practices.

"As educators," Evans stated, "we are committed to using data and evidence to inform our teaching decisions and continuously improve our practice."

Overcoming Challenges in Implementation

As the lesson progressed, Evans addressed the challenges educators may encounter when implementing change in the classroom and highlighted strategies for overcoming these obstacles.

"Overcoming challenges in implementation," Evans declared, "requires resilience, perseverance, and a willingness to learn from setbacks."

He shared examples of common challenges, such as resistance to change, lack of resources, and time constraints, and discussed how educators can address these challenges through collaboration, creativity, and support from colleagues and administrators.

"By working together," Evans concluded, "we can overcome obstacles and create learning environments where all students can thrive."

Empowering Classroom Innovation

As Evans concluded the lesson on implementing change in the classroom, he felt a sense of empowerment. By exploring the process of adapting new strategies, evaluating effectiveness, and overcoming challenges in implementation, he had equipped his students with the knowledge and strategies needed to drive innovation and improvement in their teaching practice.

His students left the classroom inspired to embrace change as an opportunity for growth and to collaborate with colleagues to create dynamic and engaging learning experiences for their students. As Evans watched them go, he knew that he was not just teaching history; he was empowering his students to become agents of change and innovation in the field of education.

With a sense of optimism, Evans looked forward to witnessing the transformative impact of classroom innovation on student learning and success in the days and weeks to come.

About the Author

Goodson Mumba is a multifaceted individual known for his diverse expertise and prolific contributions across various fields. As an infopreneur, Management Consultant, thought leader, and spiritual leader, he has inspired countless individuals through his insightful teachings and impactful writings. Mumba is also an accomplished author, with several notable works to his name, including "Understanding Corporate Worship," "The Years I Spent in a Week," "Management By Harmony," "The CEO's Diary," "Change to Change" and "Creative Thinking for results" His literary works span topics ranging from business management to personal development and spirituality, reflecting his broad range of interests and insights.

With a Master of Business Leadership (MBL) and a Bachelor of Arts in Theology (BTh), Mumba brings a unique blend of business acumen and spiritual wisdom to his work. His educational background is further enriched by a Group Diploma in Management Studies, providing him with a solid foundation in organizational dynamics and leadership principles. Additionally, Mumba holds diplomas in Education Psychology, Leadership and Management Styles, Organizational Behaviour, Financial Accounting, Economic Growth and Development, and Project Management, showcasing his commitment to continuous learning and professional development.

Mumba's expertise extends beyond traditional academic disciplines, encompassing areas such as Neuro-Linguistic Programming (NLP) and Positive Psychology. His diverse skill set is complemented by a range of certifications, including Creative Problem Solving and Decision Making, Life Coaching Fundamentals and Techniques, Professional Life Coaching, and Performance Management System Design. These certifications reflect Mumba's dedication to equipping himself with the tools and knowledge necessary to empower others and drive positive change.

As an author, Mumba's writings reflect his deep understanding of human nature, organizational dynamics, and spiritual principles. His works offer practical insights, actionable strategies, and inspirational guidance for individuals seeking personal growth, professional success, and spiritual fulfillment. Mumba's holistic approach to life and leadership resonates with readers worldwide, making him a respected figure in both the business and spiritual communities.

Overall, Goodson Mumba's diverse background, extensive knowledge, and profound insights make him a sought-after speaker, mentor, and author. His commitment to excellence, lifelong learning, and service to others continues to inspire individuals to unlock their full potential and lead lives of purpose and significance.

Goodson Mumba is renowned for initiating the concept of Management by Harmony, revolutionizing traditional management practices with a focus on balanced and holistic approaches. He has authored two influential books on this subject: "Introduction to Management by Harmony" and its sequel, "Management by Harmony."

Mumba's work has significantly impacted the field, offering innovative strategies for fostering organizational harmony and efficiency. His contributions continue to shape contemporary management theories and practices.

www.ingramcontent.com/pod-product-compliance
Lightning Source LLC
Chambersburg PA
CBHW070153230526
45471CB00002B/651